Petra Boase's Terrifyingly
Terrific T-Shirts

southwater

This edition is published by Southwater

Southwater is an imprint of Anness Publishing Limited
Hermes House, 88–89 Blackfriars Road, London SE1 8HA
tel. 020 7401 2077; fax 020 7633 9499

Published in the USA by Southwater, Anness Publishing Inc.
27 West 20th Street, New York, NY 10011; fax 212 807 6813

This edition distributed in the UK by The Manning Partnership
251–253 London Road East, Batheaston, Bath BA1 7RL
tel. 01225 852 727; fax 01225 852 852
sales@manning-partnership.co.uk

This edition distributed in the USA by National Book Network
4720 Boston Way, Langam, MD 20706
tel. 301 459 3366; fax 301 459 1705; www.nbnbooks.com

This edition distributed in Canada by General Publishing
895 Don Mills Road,400–402 Park Centre, Toronto, Ontario M3C 1W3
tel. 416 445 3333; fax 416 445 5991; www.genpub.com

This edition distributed in Australia by Sandstone Publishing
Unit 1, 360 Norton Street, Leichhardt, New South Wales 2040
tel. 02 9560 7888; fax 02 9560 7488
sales@sandstonepublishing.com.au

This edition distributed in New Zealand by Five Mile Press (NZ) Ltd
PO Box 33-1071 Takapuna, Unit 11/101-111 Diana Drive
Glenfield, Auckland 10
tel. (09) 444 4144; fax (09) 444 4518; fivemilenz@clear.net.nz

Publisher: Joanna Lorenz
Editor: Lyn Coutts
Photographer: John Freeman
Designer: Edward Kinsey

Previously published as *Creative Fun: T-Shirt Fun*

1 3 5 7 9 10 8 6 4 2

Introduction

Decorating T-shirts with fabric paints, threads and material is fun and very easy to do. In no time at all you will be creating stylish and wacky T-shirts for yourself, friends and family.

This book shows you how to prepare T-shirts as well as how to use different types of fabric paints to achieve stunning effects. It is also bursting with ideas. There are T-shirt designs for sports fans, disco dancers and animal lovers. There are even T-shirt designs for costume parties. Most of the projects are simple. A few are more difficult and use special techniques.

Once you have painted your first T-shirt, there will be no stopping you. You will be painting sweatshirts, leggings and even fabrics for your bedroom. So get to it and have fun!

Petra Boase

Contents

Materials

EMBROIDERY NEEDLE
The large eye in this needle makes it easy to thread with embroidery floss.

EMBROIDERY FLOSS
A strong, thick multi-stranded thread that is used for decorative stitching. It comes in lots of bright colors.

FABRIC CHALK
This is a special white chalk that is used for drawing outlines on dark T-shirts.

FABRIC GLUE
This glue will stick pieces of fabric together. Always use a special brush for applying fabric glue.

FABRIC MARKER
A fabric marker looks like a normal felt-tip pen but is designed to be used on fabric.

FABRIC PAINT
Fabric paint is applied to fabric and will not wash out. Always read the instructions on the container before using it.

FELT
Felt is easy to cut and will not fray. It can be bought at fabric stores or hobby shops.

FLUORESCENT FABRIC PAINT
Under ultraviolet light, this paint will glow. It comes in many bright colors.

GLITTER
This is special glitter that can be affixed to fabric with fabric glue. It is very fine, so be careful.

GLITTER FABRIC PAINT
This sparkly fabric paint comes in a tube or squeeze bottle. Always follow the instructions on the package.

HAIR DRYER
You will need a hair dryer with a low heat setting to dry puffy fabric paint.

BARRETTES
To complete one of the projects, you will need two clip-on plastic barrettes.

NEWSPAPER
To protect your work surface, cover it with newspaper.

PAINTBRUSHES
You will need fine, medium and thick paintbrushes. Always wash the brushes before changing fabric paint colors.

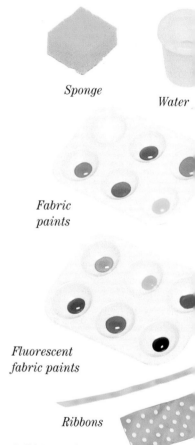

Sponge

Water

Fabric paints

Fluorescent fabric paints

Ribbons

PEARL FABRIC PAINT
This fabric paint dries with a special sheen. It comes in a squeeze bottle.

PUFFY FABRIC PAINT
When dried with a hair dryer, this paint puffs up. It comes i a squeeze bottle. Always follo the manufacturer's instructio when using puffy paint.

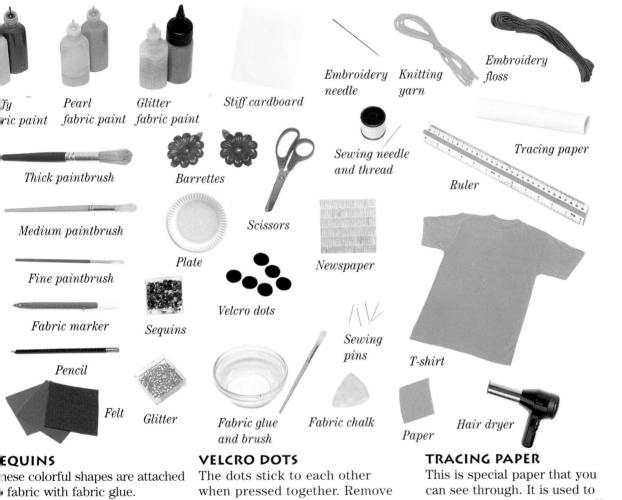

fy ric paint

Pearl fabric paint

Glitter fabric paint

Stiff cardboard

Embroidery needle

Knitting yarn

Embroidery floss

Thick paintbrush

Barrettes

Sewing needle and thread

Tracing paper

Ruler

Medium paintbrush

Scissors

Fine paintbrush

Plate

Newspaper

Fabric marker

Sequins

Velcro dots

Sewing pins

T-shirt

Pencil

Felt

Glitter

Fabric glue and brush

Fabric chalk

Paper

Hair dryer

EQUINS
hese colorful shapes are attached
fabric with fabric glue.

PONGE
u can buy an inexpensive
onge at a drugstore.
sponge dipped in fabric paint
d pressed onto fabric makes
interesting texture. A sponge
n also be used in stenciling.

VELCRO DOTS
The dots stick to each other
when pressed together. Remove
the backing to attach them
to fabric.

STIFF CARDBOARD
Pieces of cardboard are inserted
into a T-shirt to prevent fabric
paint from seeping through. Use
cardboard to make stencils, too.

TRACING PAPER
This is special paper that you
can see through. It is used to
trace templates and stencils. You
can buy it at stationery stores.

T-SHIRT
For the projects in this book you
will need cotton T-shirts. There
are designs for both short- and
long-sleeved styles.

Preparing the T-shirt

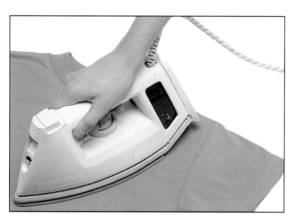

1 If you are using a new T-shirt, it is a good idea to wash and rinse it to remove excess dye. When the T-shirt is dry, ask an adult to iron it to smooth out creases.

2 To prevent fabric paint from seeping through the T-shirt, insert pieces of stiff cardboard into the body and sleeves. The pieces of cardboard should fit snugly.

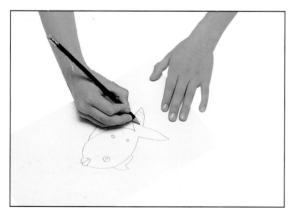

3 Draw roughs of your design on a piece of paper before drawing it on the T-shirt. Fabric marker, like fabric paints, cannot be washed out.

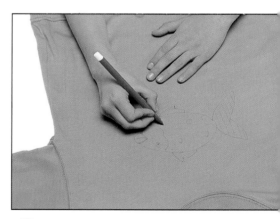

4 When you are happy with your design, draw it on the T-shirt. Use a fabric marker on light-colored T-shirts. For dark T-shirts, use fabric chalk.

Painting Tips

1 If you have only a few fabric paints, you can combine them to make other colors. or example, yellow + blue = green; yellow red = orange; red + blue = purple.

2 If you need a large quantity of a color, it is best to mix it in a pot or small bowl. Add water to your fabric paints to make them go further.

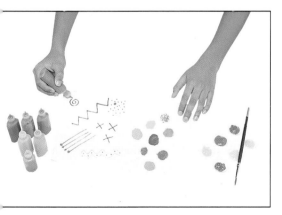

3 Before painting the T-shirt, try out the techniques and the colors on a piece f fabric. This is especially important when sing fabric paints in squeeze bottles.

4 Puffy paint only puffs up when it is dried with a hair dryer set on low heat. Before drying other fabric paints with a hair dryer, check the instructions on the paint container.

Tracing a Template

1 Place a sheet of tracing paper over the outline. Use masking tape to keep the tracing paper in position. Draw over the outline with a dark lead pencil.

2 Remove the tracing paper and turn it facedown on a sheet of paper. Use the lead pencil to draw lots of fine lines over the back of the traced outline.

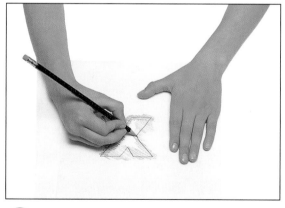

3 Place the tracing paper with the traced outline faceup on a piece of thin cardboard. Draw over the outline. The outline will be transferred to the cardboard.

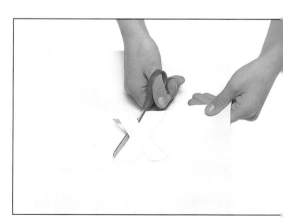

4 To make the template, cut out the outline with a pair of scissors. Place the template on the T-shirt and draw around it. Keep the template so that you can use it again.

emplates

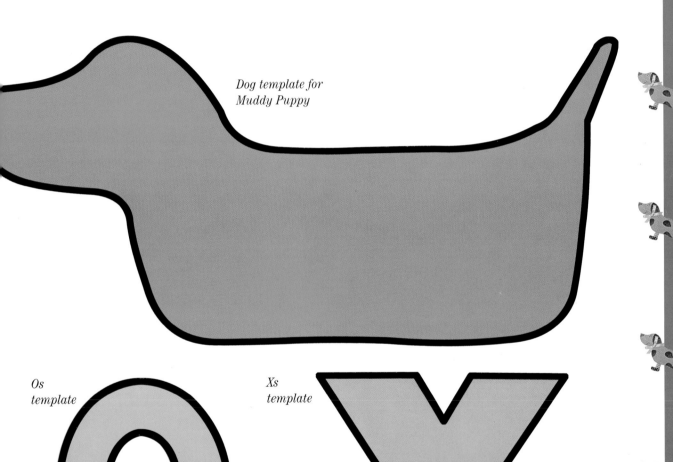

Dog template for
Muddy Puppy

Os
template

Xs
template

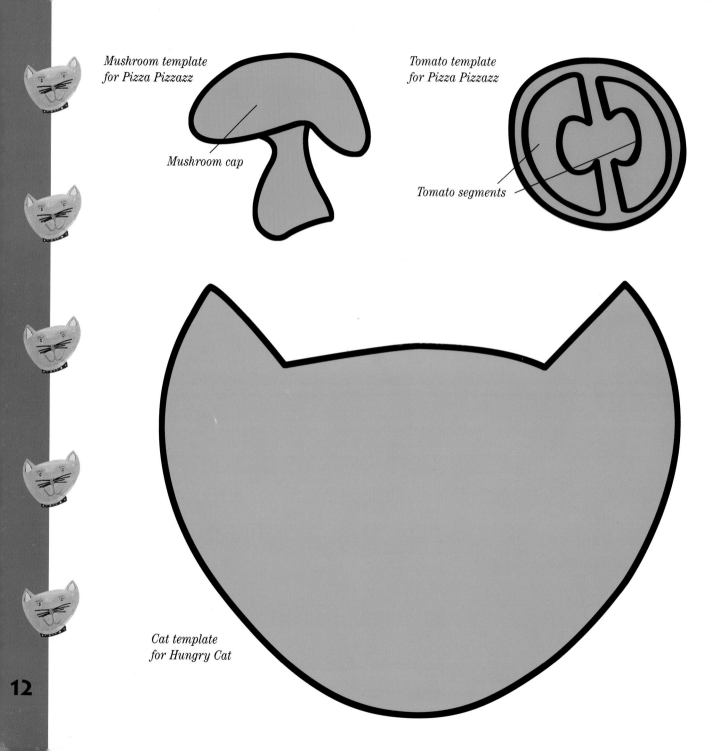

*Mushroom template
for Pizza Pizzazz*

Mushroom cap

*Tomato template
for Pizza Pizzazz*

Tomato segments

*Cat template
for Hungry Cat*

Making a Stencil

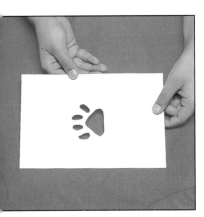

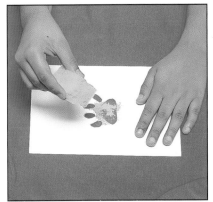

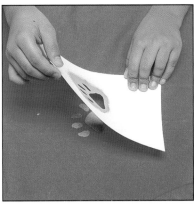

1 Follow steps 1 to 3 on page 10 to make a tracing of the outline. Use scissors to snip into the middle of the outline. Cut out the stencil following the outline.

2 Place the stencil on the T-shirt. Lightly press a dry sponge into fabric paint. Then dab the sponge on the stencil.

3 Carefully lift the stencil off the T-shirt. Before using it again, check that there are no blobs of paint on the back.

STENCILS

Fish skeleton stencil for Hungry Cat

Paws stencil for Muddy Puppy

13

Tutti-Frutti

The fruit on this T-shirt looks good enough to eat! To make the fruit look realistic, paint areas of shadow and light. Add texture with dots of pearl fabric paint and felt leaves.

YOU WILL NEED

Large sheet of cardboard
Short-sleeved T-shirt
Fabric marker
Pot of water
Fabric paint (yellow, red,
  pink, crimson)
Thick paintbrush
Pearl fabric paint (yellow, pink)
Green felt
Scissors
Fabric glue and brush

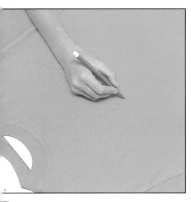

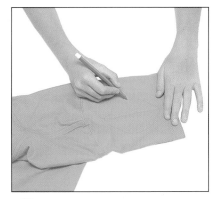

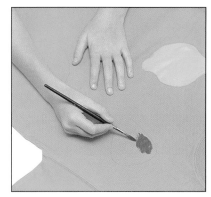

1 Insert a piece of cardboard inside the body of the T-shirt. [Us]e the fabric marker to draw the [ou]tlines of a lemon, strawberry, [ra]spberry and orange on the front of [th]e T-shirt.

2 Lay one sleeve out flat so that the seam is on the bottom. Insert a piece of cardboard into the sleeve. Use the fabric marker to draw a piece of fruit on the sleeve. Repeat on the other sleeve.

3 Use the thick brush to paint the fruit on the front of the T-shirt with fabric paint. To make orange, combine red and yellow. Let the fabric paint dry before painting the fruit on the sleeves.

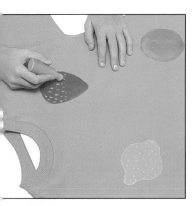

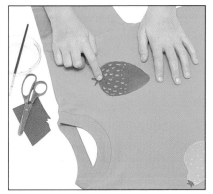

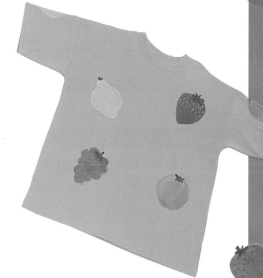

4 To add texture to the orange, strawberry and lemon, make [do]ts using yellow and pink pearl [fab]ric paint. Let dry before doing [the] same to the pieces of fruit [on] the sleeves.

5 Use the fabric marker to draw the outlines of leaves on the green felt. Cut out the leaves and glue them on the fruit with fabric glue. Let dry before trying on your Tutti-Frutti T-shirt.

Muddy Puppy

Oh, no! Someone has let a puppy walk all over this T-shirt with its muddy paws! Surely such a bad puppy does not deserve a big, juicy bone! To prevent the puppy from covering everything in the house with mud, it has been given a fancy pair of socks to wear.

YOU WILL NEED
2 sheets of cardboard
Short-sleeved T-shirt
Pencil
Tracing paper
Scissors
Fabric marker
Pot of water
Fabric paint (brown, black, white,
  turquoise, red, pale blue, yellow)
Fine and thick paintbrushes
Narrow yellow ribbon
Fabric glue and brush
Sponge

1 Insert pieces of cardboard inside the body and sleeves of the T-shirt. Trace the template for the dog on page 11. Place the template on the front of the T-shirt. Draw around it using the fabric marker.

2 Paint the dog brown using the thick brush. If you do not have brown paint, make some by mixing together blue, red and yellow. Make light and dark shades of brown by adding white or black. Let dry before starting the next step.

Use the fine brush to paint black spots on the body. ...ntinue using the black to paint ...ear, tail, shoes and bone. Add ...tures to the face and decorate ... socks and shoes. Paint a collar.

4 Let the paint dry before starting this step. Tie the piece of ribbon into a small bow. Trim the ends. Attach the bow to the collar with fabric glue. Hold the bow in position until the glue is dry.

5 Trace the paw-print stencil on page 13. Cut out the stencil as shown. Turn the T-shirt over so that the back is facing you. Make sure that the pieces of cardboard are still in position inside the T-shirt.

Place the stencil on the T-shirt. Hold it in position and ... a sponge to dab light and dark ...wn fabric paint on the stencil. ...t off the stencil. Repeat until the ...ck of the T-shirt is covered with ...ddy paw prints.

17

Crazy Spiral

This wacky T-shirt is easy to make if you are new to fabric painting. Draw the outline of the spiral as large as you can to make it easy to paint and decorate. You can add smaller spirals to the design or paint a spiral on the back of your T-shirt, too.

YOU WILL NEED

Large sheet of cardboard
Short-sleeved T-shirt
Fabric marker
Pot of water
Fabric paint (black, orange, yellow,
  light blue, green)
Fine, medium and thick paintbrushes
Pearl fabric paint (yellow,
  orange, purple)
Glitter fabric paint (green, purple)

18

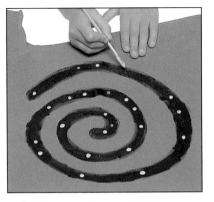

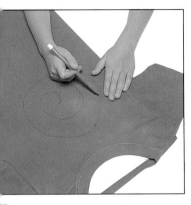

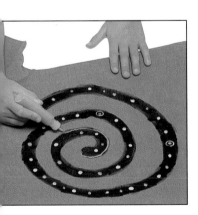

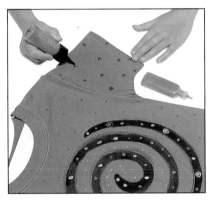

1 Insert pieces of cardboard inside the body and sleeves of the T-shirt. Use the fabric marker to draw a large curly spiral on the front of the T-shirt.

2 Paint the spiral with black fabric paint using the thick brush. Let the paint dry thoroughly before starting the next step.

3 Decorate the spiral with orange, yellow, light blue and green dots of fabric paint. Do this using the medium brush. Let the paint dry thoroughly.

4 Draw circles around some of the dots using yellow pearl fabric paint. Go around the outline of the spiral with orange and purple pearl fabric paint. Let the paint dry.

5 Make dots of yellow pearl fabric paint inside the spiral. Use glitter fabric paint to cover the front of the T-shirt with green dots. To finish, dot the sleeves with purple glitter fabric paint.

Swirly Spots and Dots

This is the perfect T-shirt to wear when you are out with your friends for a day of wild adventures. The design is very simple to draw, and you can use as many or as few colors as you like. It is important to let the fabric paint dry before you start decorating the circles with puffy and glitter fabric paints.

YOU WILL NEED
Large sheet of cardboard
Short-sleeved T-shirt
Fabric marker
Pot of water
Medium paintbrush

Fabric paint (red, black, pink, blue, white)
Puffy fabric paint (purpl, red, yellow, orange, blu
Hair dryer
Glitter fabric paint (silve

1 Insert pieces of cardboard inside the body and sleeves of the T-shirt. Use the fabric marker to draw large circles on the front of the T-shirt. Draw circles on the sleeves as well.

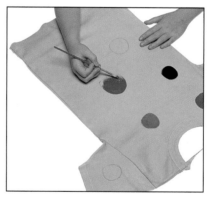

2 Use the medium brush to paint the circles different colors. Do not forget to wash the brush when changing colors. Let the fabric paint dry thoroughly before starting the next step.

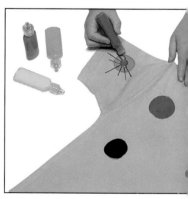

3 Use purple, red, yellow, orang and blue puffy fabric paint to decorate some of the circles with swirls, lines, dots and spots. To make the puffy fabric paint puff up, dry it with the hair dryer.

HANDY HINT

When using puffy or glitter fabric paints in squeeze bottles, always keep the nozzle moving smoothly and evenly over your design. If you let the nozzle stay in one place for too long, the paint will form blobs.

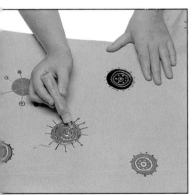

4 To make your T-shirt even more dazzling, decorate the remaining circles with silver glitter fabric paint. To finish, add glitter fabric paint to those circles already decorated with puffy fabric paint.

21

Bug Collector

Eek! Don't look now, but there are spiders and insects crawling all over you. The Bug Collector T-shirt is not for the squeamish—it is for the enthusiastic critter collector who really wants to bug his friends and family. You can invent your own creatures or, better still, copy them from real life!

YOU WILL NEED

Large sheet of cardboard
Long-sleeved T-shirt
Fabric marker
Pot of water
Fabric paint (black, red)

Fine and medium
*   paintbrushes*
Black fabric paint or
*   pearl fabric paint in*
*   squeeze bottles*

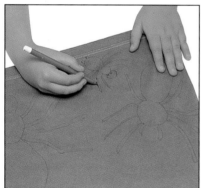

1 Insert pieces of cardboard inside the body and sleeves of the T-shirt. Use the fabric marker to draw three large spiders on the front of the T-shirt. Draw two or three spiders on each sleeve.

2 Use the medium brush and black fabric paint to paint the spiders' heads, bodies and fangs. To paint the black jointed legs, use the fine brush. Wash the brush before painting the spiders' eyes red.

3 Dip a finger into black fabric paint and press it onto the T-shirt to make the body and head of a small insect. Repeat until you have covered the front of the T-shirt with bugs. Let dry.

ANDY HINT

make repeated designs, like the
all spiders, you could make a
mp with a halved potato. Etch
e shape into a cut surface of the
tato with a blunt pencil. Ask an
ult to cut away the potato from
ound the shape with a sharp
ife. Dip the stamp into fabric
int and press it onto the T-shirt.

To paint legs on the creatures,
use black fabric paint or
earl fabric paint in squeeze
ottles. Let the paint dry. If
esired, you can paint more
gs on the back of the T-shirt.

Cactus Flower

This cactus has been painted on a yellow T-shirt because cacti grow in deserts. Even though rain rarely falls in the desert, a cactus can live for more than 100 years! It has prickly spines so that it does not lose moisture and to prevent animals from eating its juicy trunk. When it does rain, the cactus bursts into flower.

YOU WILL NEED

Sheet of cardboard
Scissors
Short-sleeved T-shirt
Fabric marker
Pot of water
Medium paintbrush

Fabric paint (red, blue, pink, dark and light green, yellow)
Green embroidery floss
Embroidery needle

1 Insert pieces of cardboard into the body and sleeves of the T-shirt. Use the fabric marker to draw a flowering cactus and plant pot on the front of the T-shirt. Draw a decorative pattern around the pot.

2 Draw zigzag patterns along the bottom of the T-shirt, the edges of the sleeves and around the collar with the marker. Use the medium brush to paint the pattern with red and blue fabric paint.

3 Paint the pot red and the flower pink, then paint the border around the pot blue. Roughly paint the cactus with light and dark green fabric paint. To make light green, add yellow to dark green.

24

Let the fabric paint dry. Thread the needle with the [flo]ss. Tie a knot at the end. Push the [ne]edle and thread in and out of the [fro]nt of the T-shirt to sew large [sti]tches onto the cactus. These are [th]e cactus's prickly spikes. Secure [th]e thread with a knot to finish.

[H]ANDY HINT

[Be]fore decorating the back [of] a T-shirt, the front must be [dr]y. You can speed up the drying [by] using a hair dryer, but before [do]ing so, check the instructions [on] the fabric paint containers. [Wh]en you turn the T-shirt over, [ma]ke sure that the pieces of [ca]rdboard are still in position.

Space Trekker

This T-shirt goes where no other T-shirt has gone before. Its fluorescent yellow afterburners will be seen by alien beings in all the far-flung galaxies. But all space trekkers should make sure that they know how to get back to Planet Earth!

YOU WILL NEED

Large sheet of cardboard
Dark short-sleeved T-shirt
Fabric chalk
Pot of water
Fabric paint (dark blue, light blue, black, red, fluorescent yellow, silver)
Medium and thick paintbrushes
Pearl fabric paint (red)

Insert pieces of cardboard inside the body and sleeves of the T-shirt. Use the fabric chalk to draw the outlines of planets, stars and a rocket. Draw only the end of the rocket and its thrusters on the front of the T-shirt.

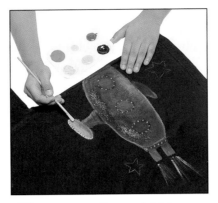

Use the medium and thick brushes to paint the rocket with dark blue, light blue, black and red fabric paint. Use fluorescent yellow fabric paint for rivets and the glow of the afterburners. Paint the top of the rocket with silver fabric paint.

Paint the stars with silver fabric paint. Use plain and fluorescent fabric paints for the planets. When the paint is dry, make a ring around each planet with red pearl fabric paint. Use the pearl fabric paint to add extra details to the rocket.

To make galaxies of stars, dip the thick brush in yellow fluorescent fabric paint and then flick the brush at the T-shirt. Droplets of paint will scatter all over it. Repeat until the T-shirt is aglow with dazzling stars. Let the paint dry before starting the next step.

Turn the T-shirt over, making sure that the pieces of cardboard are still in position. Use the fabric chalk to draw the front of the rocket so that it lines up with the section on the front. Paint and decorate the rocket and the galaxy of stars as before.

Sea Life Fantasy

When you look at this T-shirt you can almost smell the salty air, hear the crash of the waves and see the schools of brightly colored fish darting around in a pale blue ocean. In this design there are only two species of marine life, but you could also add some crabs, shells, coral and bright green fronds of seaweed.

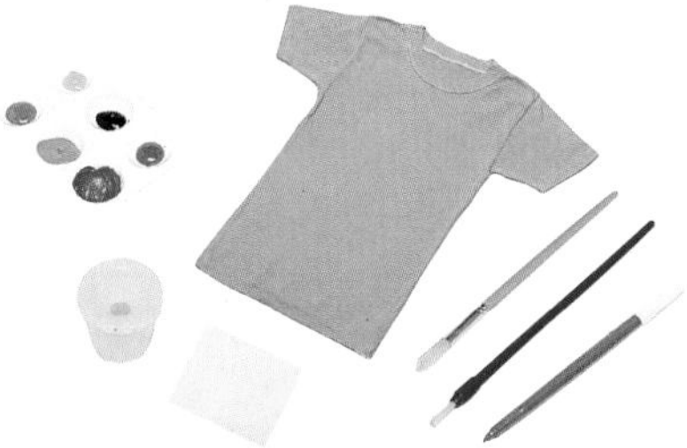

YOU WILL NEED

Large sheet of cardboard
Short-sleeved blue T-shirt
Fabric marker
Pot of water
Fabric paint (light blue, dark blue,
*   yellow, pink, red, black)*
Fine and thick paintbrushes

1 Insert the piece of cardboard inside the body of the T-shirt. [Us]e the fabric marker to draw the [ou]tlines of the fish, starfish and [wa]ves on the front of the T-shirt.

2 Paint the waves with light and dark blue fabric paint using the thick brush. Do not worry if the paint does not go on smoothly—an uneven texture will look more realistic.

3 Paint the fish in shades of blue, green, pink and red. The green can be made by mixing yellow and blue. Use the fine brush to paint the lips and eyes. Paint black bubbles coming from their mouths. Mix red and yellow to make orange. Paint the starfish with the orange paint.

4 Let the fabric paint dry thoroughly. Turn the T-shirt [ov]er, making sure that the piece of [ca]rdboard is still in position. Use the [fa]bric marker to draw another fish [on] the back of the T-shirt. Continue [th]e pattern of the waves.

5 Use the thick brush to paint the waves with light and dark blue fabric paint. Wash the brush before painting the fish pink with yellow spots. Paint features on the fish's face and bubbles coming from its mouth.

Basketballer

If you can slam-dunk and dribble, then this is the T-shirt design for you. Why not get together with some friends to make a basketball team? You can have a different number each and choose your own team colors.

YOU WILL NEED

Large sheet of cardboard
Short-sleeved T-shirt
Fabric marker
Pot of water
Fabric paint (red, black)
Medium and thick paintbrushes

1 Insert pieces of cardboard inside the body and sleeves of e T-shirt. Use the fabric marker to aw the outline of the number 7 on e front. Draw two bands along the lge of each sleeve front.

2 Use the thick brush to fill in the outline of the number with red fabric paint. Try to apply the paint evenly and smoothly. Let the paint dry thoroughly before starting the next step.

3 Paint a narrow line around the number using the medium brush and black fabric paint. You can change these colors to match your favorite team if you like. Let the paint dry.

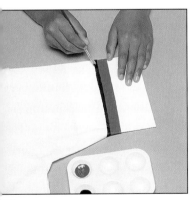
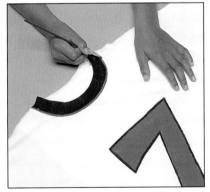

4 Wash the thick brush and use it to fill in the bottom outline each sleeve with red fabric paint. hen the fabric paint is dry, use the edium brush to paint the narrower ack line.

5 Paint the ribbing around the neck of the T-shirt with black fabric paint. When dry, use the medium brush to paint the narrow red line. Let dry. Turn the T-shirt over and repeat steps 1 to 5.

HANDY HINT
Use a ruler to help you make the outlines for the number and the bands straight.

Hawaiian Dancer

Aloha! Welcome to a tropical luau. Luau is the Hawaiian word for party, and the traditional dress for a luau dancer is a grass skirt with a lei of flowers around the neck. Wear some flowers in your hair and around your wrist and you are ready to do the hula dance.

YOU WILL NEED

Large sheet of cardboard
Long, sleeveless flesh-colored T-shirt
Fabric marker
Pot of water
Fabric paint (yellow, pink, orange, red, white, green)
Fine and thick paintbrushes

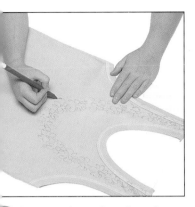

1 Insert a piece of cardboard inside the body of the T-shirt. [Us]e the fabric marker to draw the [out]line of the lei of flowers, belly [bu]tton and grass skirt on the front [of] the T-shirt.

2 Use the fine brush to paint the lei of yellow, pink, orange and red flowers. Add white to these colors to make lighter shades. Let the paint dry.

3 To paint the grass skirt, use the thick brush and different shades of green fabric paint. You can make different shades of green by adding yellow or white.

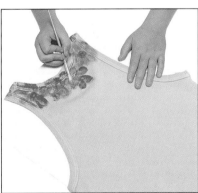

4 To make the belly button, use the fine brush and pink fabric [pa]int. Let the fabric paint dry. Turn [th]e T-shirt over, making sure that the [pie]ce of cardboard is still in position.

5 Use the fabric marker to draw the outline of the lei and the skirt. Paint these as before. When the paint has dried, you are ready to hula!

Bones, the Skeleton

This spooky T-shirt is perfect for a Halloween costume party. All you need to complete your nightmare outfit is a tight-fitting black cap, black leggings and a pair of black gloves. To make up your face as a skull, use white face paint or talcum powder and black eye shadow.

YOU WILL NEED

Large sheet of cardboard
Long-sleeved black T-shirt
Fabric chalk

Pot of water
Fabric paint (white)
Thick paintbrush

① Insert pieces of cardboard inside the body and sleeves of the T-shirt. Use the fabric chalk to draw the outlines of the shoulder blades, rib cage, spine and hips.

② Use the fabric chalk to draw the outlines of the upper and lower arm bones on the front of both sleeves. These bones should be long and thick.

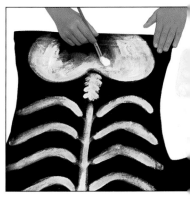

③ Use the thick brush to paint the bones on the front of the T-shirt with white fabric paint. To make them really white, use two coats. Let the paint dry between coats.

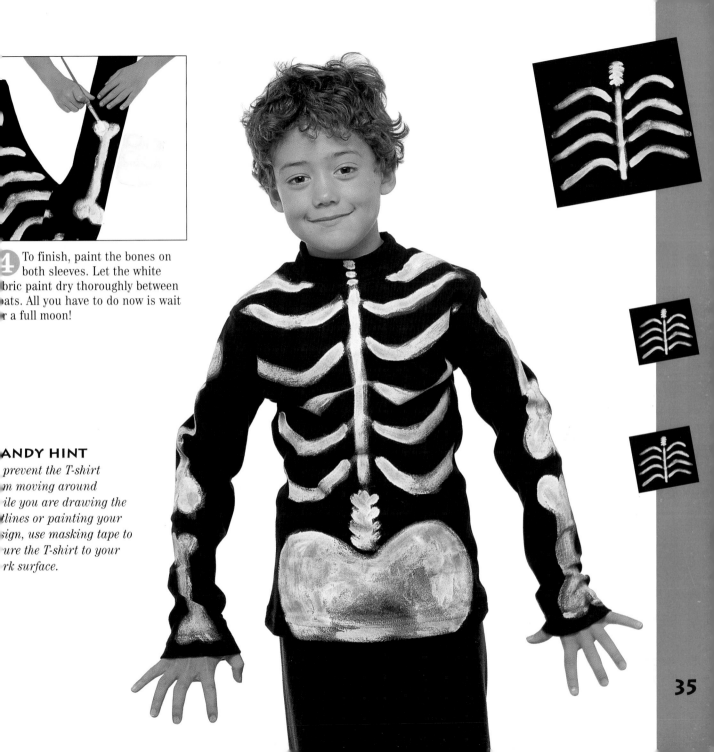

4 To finish, paint the bones on both sleeves. Let the white [fa]bric paint dry thoroughly between [co]ats. All you have to do now is wait [fo]r a full moon!

[To] prevent the T-shirt [fro]m moving around [wh]ile you are drawing the [out]lines or painting your [de]sign, use masking tape to [sec]ure the T-shirt to your [wo]rk surface.

35

Pockets of Fun

If you wear this clever T-shirt you will no longer lose or leave at home all your favorite odds and ends. You can even use one of the pockets to keep your allowance safe! Why not make a matching T-shirt as a present for your best friend?

YOU WILL NEED

Scissors
Orange, mauve, green
and blue felt
Fabric glue and brush
Short-sleeved T-shirt
Straight pins
Embroidery needle
Yellow, orange and green
embroidery floss
Fabric marker
Large sheet of cardboard
Pot of water
Fabric paint (light blue, pink,
yellow, orange, red, gold)
Medium paintbrush

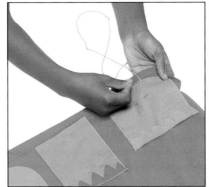

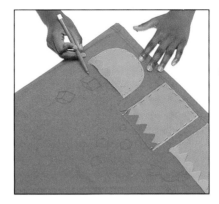

1 Cut three pockets and three decorative strips from the ange, mauve, green and blue felt. e strips must be long enough to fit ong the top edge of each pocket. ue a strip onto the top of each cket with fabric glue.

2 Position the pockets along the bottom of the T-shirt with pins. Thread the needle with embroidery floss and tie a knot in the end. Use floss that is a different color from the pocket. Sew the pockets onto the front of the T-shirt using big stitches.

3 Use the fabric marker to draw the outlines of candy, coins and dice just above each pocket. Here are ideas for other items you could draw: pencils, erasers, jewelry, sunglasses, favorite toys, lipstick and barrettes.

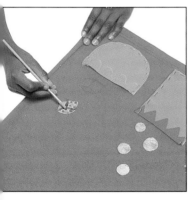

HANDY HINT
Place a piece of cardboard inside the body of the T-shirt when sewing on the pockets. This will prevent you from accidentally sewing the front and the back of the T-shirt together.

4 Insert a piece of cardboard into the body of the T-shirt. Paint e candy wrappers and dice in bright lors. Use gold fabric paint for the ins. When the paint is dry, put on ur T-shirt and fill the pockets with your treasures!

Modern Artist

Modern art has never been so much fun or so easy. To make this colorful, paint-splattered T-shirt, you just have to flick a paintbrush loaded with runny fabric paint all over the T-shirt. Try not to splatter paint over walls, furniture and members of your family—it could mean an early end to a promising artistic career!

YOU WILL NEED
Newspaper
Large sheet of cardboard
Short-sleeved T-shirt
Pot of water
Fabric paint (yellow, orange, red, green, blue)
Thick paintbrush

1 Cover the work surface with newspaper. Insert pieces of cardboard inside the body and sleeves of the T-shirt. Add water to the fabric paints to make them runny. Dip the thick brush into the yellow fabric paint and flick it at the T-shirt.

2 Wash the brush thoroughly before changing colors. Dip the clean brush into the orange fabric paint and flick the brush at the T-shirt.

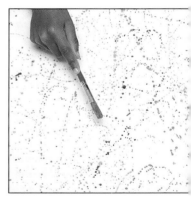

3 Do the same with the red, green and blue fabric paints. You can flick more colors if you like. Let the paint dry before wearing your T-shirt.

ANDY HINT

[Wh]en splatter painting, start with the lightest color and [the]n apply the darker colors. The last color that you [spl]atter on the T-shirt should be the darkest. To make a [fin]er splatter, drag a plastic ruler across the bristles of [a p]ailbrush that has been dipped in fabric paint. [Alw]ays pull the ruler toward you, unless you want to [spl]atter yourself!

Disco Dazzler

Wear this wild T-shirt to be the center of attention. The patterns will positively glow in the dark under ultraviolet light. This is because they have been painted using fluorescent fabric paint. To be the ultimate disco dazzler, paint the names of your favorite bands on the back of the T-shirt.

YOU WILL NEED
Large sheet of cardboard
Short-sleeved black T-shirt
Fabric chalk
Pot of water
Medium paintbrush

Fluorescent fabric paint (yellow, blue, pink, orange, green)
Puffy fabric paint (orange, yellow, purple, red)
Hair dryer

1 Insert pieces of cardboard inside the body and sleeves of the T-shirt. Use the fabric chalk to draw the outlines of triangles, spirals and zigzag patterns all over the front and the sleeves of the T-shirt.

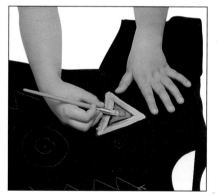

2 Use fluorescent yellow, blue, pink, orange and green fabric paint to fill in the outlines. To make other colors, simply combine different colors. Let the fabric paint dry.

3 Decorate the T-shirt with dots and squiggles of orange, yellow, purple and red puffy paint. To make the puffy fabric paint puff up, dry it with a hair dryer. Set the hair dryer to its coolest setting.

4 Decorate the bottom of the T-shirt with a zigzag pattern using puffy fabric paint. Once again, use the hair dryer on its coolest temperature to dry the puffy paint.

Hairdo Suzie

How will you do Suzie's hair today? Will it be in braids, pigtails or hanging loose? You could even do her hair in lots of fine braids with beads threaded onto the ends! Instead of barrettes, tie Suzie's hair with brightly colored ribbons.

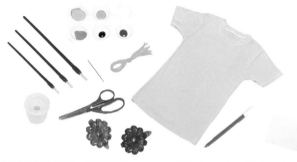

YOU WILL NEED

Large sheet of cardboard
Short-sleeved T-shirt
Fabric marker
Pot of water
Fine, medium and thick paintbrushes

Fabric paint (light pink, dark pink, white, red, blue, black)
Scissors
Yellow yarn
Embroidery needle
2 barrettes

1 Insert a piece of cardboard inside the body of the T-shirt. Use the fabric marker to draw the outline of the face and neck on the T-shirt. Hairdo Suzie's head needs to be about 6 inches long.

2 Use the thick brush to fill in the outline with light pink fabric paint. Use the dark pink to make Suzie's rosy cheeks. Let the paint dry thoroughly before starting the next step.

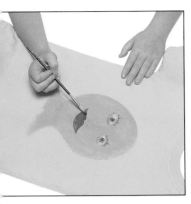

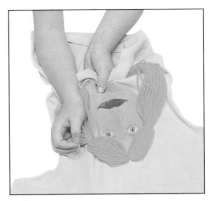

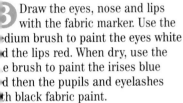
Draw the eyes, nose and lips with the fabric marker. Use the medium brush to paint the eyes white and the lips red. When dry, use the fine brush to paint the irises blue and then the pupils and eyelashes with black fabric paint.

To make the hair, you will need 40 strands of yarn, each 25 inches long. Lay out the strands so the ends are even. Tie them together in the middle with a piece of yarn.

Thread the embroidery needle with a long length of yarn and knot the end. Place the hair on the head. Sew it onto the T-shirt with stitches at the top and at the sides. Put the hair into pigtails with the barrettes.

HANDY HINT

To keep Hairdo Suzie's golden locks in good condition, this T-shirt should be hand washed and laid flat to dry. Do not forget to remove barrettes and ribbons before washing the T-shirt.

Busy Executive

When is a T-shirt not a T-shirt? When it is painted to look like an executive's shirt and tie. Dressing up a plain T-shirt to look like something else is easy. You could paint a police officer's jacket and include details like the badge, whistle and radio, or a doctor's coat complete with stethoscope. There is no end to the mischief your disguises could cause!

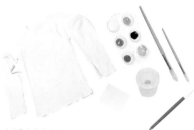

YOU WILL NEED

Large sheet of cardboard
Long-sleeved T-shirt
Fabric marker
Pot of water
Fabric paint (pale blue, black, orange,
  white, red, gold)
Fine and medium paintbrushes

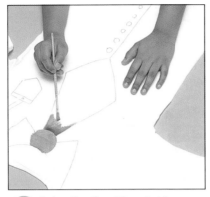

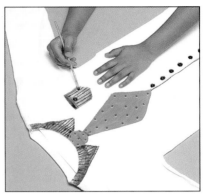

1 Insert pieces of cardboard inside the body and sleeves the T-shirt. Use the fabric marker draw the outlines of the collar, irtfront, buttons, tie and pocket on e front of the T-shirt. Draw a watch one sleeve.

2 Paint the tie with pale blue fabric paint using the medium brush. Use a darker shade of blue under the knot of the tie so that it stands out. When dry, decorate the tie with dots of orange fabric paint.

3 Paint the buttons and shirtfront dark blue. Use a lighter blue for the collar and pocket. Let dry before painting dark blue stripes on the collar and pocket. Paint a button on the pocket.

HANDY HINT

Copy pictures of businesspeople, police officers and doctors from magazines so that your T-shirt design is really accurate. Color pictures will make it easy for you to choose exactly the right colors.

4 Mix white and black fabric paint to make gray. Paint the atch face gray. When dry, paint e red outline and black hands. To ake the watch look valuable, paint e watchband with gold fabric aint. Let dry.

5 Turn the T-shirt over, making sure that the pieces of cardboard are still in place. Use the fabric marker to draw the outline of the collar on the back of the T-shirt. Paint the collar as before. To finish, draw and paint the rest of the watchband.

Tic-tac-toe

This T-shirt is a lot of fun. Well, it's not often that an item of clothing doubles as a game, is it? Wear it when you are traveling long distances and you will never be bored. Before washing the T-shirt, remove the Xs and Os.

YOU WILL NEED

2 sheets of cardboard
Short-sleeved T-shirt
Ruler
Fabric marker
Pearl fabric paint
  (orange)
Pencil

Tracing paper
Paper
Scissors
Blue and red felt
Fabric glue and brush
9 Velcro dots

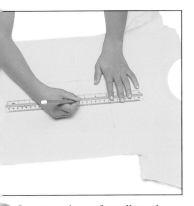

1 Insert a piece of cardboard inside the body of the T-shirt. [Us]e a ruler and fabric marker to [me]asure and draw the tic-tac-toe [gri]d. The lines should be 10 inches [lon]g and 3 inches apart.

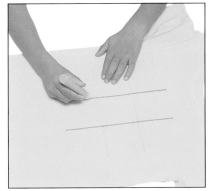

2 Go over the lines with orange pearl fabric paint in a squeezable tube. Move the tube evenly along the lines—otherwise the pearl paint will form blobs. Let the paint dry thoroughly.

3 To make the Xs and Os templates, see page 11. Place the templates on the felt and draw around them. You will need four red Os and four blue Xs. Cut out the shapes. Also cut out four small blue ovals and glue these onto the Os with fabric glue.

4 Remove the backing from one side of a Velcro dot. Press [th]e sticky surface onto the back of [on]e of the felt shapes. Repeat for all [th]e shapes.

5 Remove the backing from the remaining dots and press them into the center of each square on the grid. You are now ready to play tic-tac-toe!

Pizza Pizzazz

This T-shirt is the ultimate in takeout food. Wherever you go, you take the pizza with you! This mushroom and tomato pizza is just the first course. Why not make a sausage pizza as well!

YOU WILL NEED

2 sheets of cardboard
Short-sleeved T-shirt
Plate
Fabric marker
Pot of water
Fabric paint (red)
Thick paintbrush
Pearl fabric paint (gold)
Pencil
Tracing paper
Scissors
Brown, light brown and red felt
Fabric glue and brush
10 Velcro dots

1 Insert a piece of cardboard inside the body of the T-shirt. Place a medium-size plate in the center of the T-shirt and draw around it with the fabric marker. This is the pizza crust.

2 Use the thick brush to cover the pizza base with a tomato-red fabric paint. Let this dry before painting the crispy crust with gold pearl paint. This pizza is looking very delicious!

3 Make the templates for the mushrooms and the tomatoes on page 12. Place the mushroom template on the felt and draw around it. You will need to draw five whole brown mushrooms and five pale brown mushroom caps. Cut out the pieces. Glue the mushroom caps onto the whole mushrooms with fabric glue.

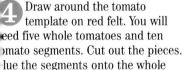

4 Draw around the tomato template on red felt. You will need five whole tomatoes and ten tomato segments. Cut out the pieces. Glue the segments onto the whole tomatoes with fabric glue. Paint the seeds using the gold pearl paint.

5 Remove the backing from the Velcro dots. Press five dots around the edge of the pizza. Press dots on the back of the mushrooms and tomatoes. What would you like—a mushroom pizza or a tomato pizza?

HANDY HINT
If you cannot find Velcro dots with self-adhesive backing, you can use fabric glue to stick the dots to the T-shirt and to the felt shapes. Remove the felt shapes before washing this T-shirt.

Really Wild

It is time to go on safari, but you must tread softly so that the real kings of the jungle do not see you! Majestic lions and ferocious tigers may not like human impersonators prowling on their territory.

YOU WILL NEED

Large sheet of cardboard
Long-sleeved T-shirt
Fabric marker
Pot of water
Fabric paint (brown, red, orange, yellow, black)
Thick paintbrush

1 Insert a piece of cardboard inside the body of the T-shirt. Use the fabric marker to draw the outlines of the tiger stripes on the front of the T-shirt.

2 Paint the stripes using brown, red, orange, yellow and black fabric paints. It does not matter if the stripes are uneven, as this will make them look more realistic.

3 When the paint is dry, turn the T-shirt over. Check that the cardboard is still in place. Use the marker to draw more stripes and a tail onto the back of the T-shirt.

4 Use the same colors as before to paint the stripes and tail. Let your T-shirt dry before you start prowling and growling in it.

Glitzy Stars

This twinkling T-shirt is perfect for a party or special occasion. The glitter and sequins will make the stars sparkle under lights. Fabric glitter is specially made for use on fabrics. It can be bought at hobby shops and craft stores. Ordinary craft glitter should not be used for this design.

YOU WILL NEED

Large sheet of cardboard
Short-sleeved T-shirt
Fabric marker
Pot of water
Fabric paint (blue, yellow, white, red, pink, green)
Fine paintbrush
Pearl fabric paint (yellow)
Glitter fabric paint (gold)
Fabric glue and brush
Fabric glitter
Sequins
Sheet of paper

1 Insert a piece of cardboard inside the body of the T-shirt. e the fabric marker to draw the tlines of stars all over the front the T-shirt.

2 Use the fine brush to paint the stars with blue, green, red, yellow and pink fabric paints. To make lighter shades of these colors, add white.

3 Paint around the edges of the stars with yellow pearl fabric paint and gold glitter fabric paint. Decorate the stars with dots and spots of yellow and gold.

4 Now it is time to really add some sparkle to this T-shirt. int the stars with fabric glue. hile the glue is still wet, sprinkle fabric glitter and sequins. Let e glue dry.

5 To remove excess fabric glitter and sequins, gently shake the T-shirt over a piece of paper. Carefully fold the paper to form a spout and pour the fabric glitter and sequins back into their containers.

All-weather T-shirt

This T-shirt can be designed to match any weather forecast—except, maybe gale-force winds. If rain is coming then paint a rainbow on the back and flashes of lightning on the front. The perfect winter T-shirt could be covered with snowflakes.

YOU WILL NEED
Large piece of cardboard
Long-sleeved, light blue T-shir
Plate
Fabric marker
Pot of water
Fabric paint (yellow, red, wh
Medium and thick paintbrush
Sponge

HANDY HINT
To make the clouds light and wispy, do not load too much paint on the sponge. To get the interesting texture of the sponge, press the sponge gently onto the T-shirt.

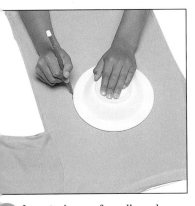

1 Insert pieces of cardboard inside the body and sleeves of [th]e T-shirt. Use the fabric marker to [dr]aw around a medium-size plate on [th]e back of the T-shirt.

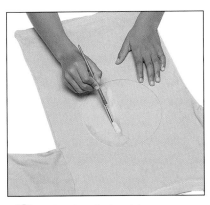

2 Paint the circle with a sunny yellow fabric paint. Do this with the thick brush. Let dry. Use the marker to give the sun a smiling face and lots of rays.

3 Mix red and yellow fabric paints to make shades of orange. Use this to paint the eyes, mouth and rays.

4 When the fabric paint is dry, turn the T-shirt over. Check [th]at the pieces of cardboard are still [in] place. Lightly dip the dry sponge [in]to white fabric paint.

5 Dab the sponge on the front of the T-shirt to make a wispy cloud. Repeat until the front of the T-shirt and sleeves are covered. Let the paint dry.

Birthday Present

Why not make this T-shirt as a gift for a friend's birthday? Your friend could wear it to his or her own party! It is important that the painted ribbon match the real ribbon. To achieve this, you may have to combine fabric paints to make exactly the right color.

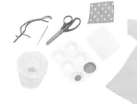

YOU WILL NEED

Large sheet of cardboard
Short-sleeved T-shirt
Ruler
Fabric marker
Pot of water
Fabric paint (green,
    white, pink)

Medium and thick
    paintbrushes
15–20 inches of wide
    green ribbon
Scissors
Green thread
Needle

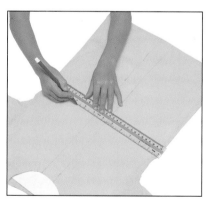

1 Insert pieces of cardboard inside the body and sleeves of the T-shirt. Use the ruler and fabric marker to draw two parallel lines down the center of the T-shirt and two parallel lines across the T-shirt, as shown.

2 Paint the area inside the lines with green fabric paint. Do this with the thick brush. These are the ribbons on the present. Make the edges of the ribbon as straight as possible. Let dry.

3 Use the medium brush to decorate the painted ribbon with small dots of white fabric paint. Wash the brush. Cover the rest of the T-shirt with larger pink dots. Let dry.

Tie the length of ribbon into a big bow. Trim the ends. Thread [th]e needle and tie a knot in the end [of] the thread. Position the bow [wh]ere the painted ribbons cross and [se]w it in place. Keep sewing until the [bo]w is securely attached.

[H]ANDY HINT

[Tr]y adding a little water to [fa]bric paint—it makes the paint [ea]sier to apply and changes the [co]lor slightly. The more water [yo]u add, the lighter the color [wi]ll become. Do not make the [fa]bric paint too runny, or it [wi]ll drip all over the place.

57

Hungry Cat

This hungry cat is dreaming of a seafood feast. If the dream does not come true, the cat's contented purr will become a moaning meow. Does the cat get its wish? Look at the back of the T-shirt to find out. Oh dear, poor little fish!

YOU WILL NEED

2 sheets of cardboard
Short-sleeved T-shirt
Pencil
Tracing paper
Scissors
Fabric marker
Pot of water
Fabric paint (blue, white, black, red, yellow, orange, pink)
Medium and thick paintbrushes
Sponge
Black embroidery floss
Embroidery needle

1 Insert a piece of cardboard inside the body of the T-shirt. Make the cat template on page 12. Place the template on the front of the T-shirt and draw around it with the fabric marker.

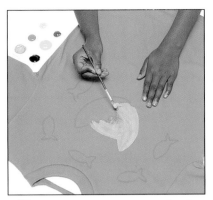

2 Use the thick brush to paint the cat's face with blue-gray fabric paint. To make this color, mix blue, white and black fabric paints. Add more white to this color to paint the cat's markings.

3 Draw five fish using the fabric marker. Paint the fish different colors. This hungry cat is dreaming of its seafood supper, so give it a happy and contented face. Paint and decorate the cat's fancy collar.

4 Make the stencil for the fish skeleton on page 13. When the fabric paint is dry, turn the T-shirt over. Place the stencil on the back of the T-shirt and dab it with a sponge dipped in red fabric paint. Lift off the stencil. Stencil four more skeletons in different colors.

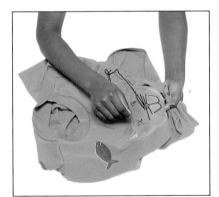

5 When the fabric paint is dry, remove the cardboard and turn the T-shirt over again. Thread the needle with black embroidery floss and tie a knot at the end. Sew four long stitches on either side of the cat's nose to make the whiskers.

59

Optical Illusion

If you look at this crazy T-shirt for too long you are bound to feel dizzy. There was a Dutch artist called M. C. Escher who became very famous for his paintings of bizarre optical illusions. In his paintings, nothing was ever what it seemed—water flowed uphill and a school of fish would become a flock of birds before your eyes.

YOU WILL NEED
Large sheet of cardboard
Short-sleeved T-shirt
Fabric marker
Pearl fabric paint (black)

1 Insert a piece of cardboard inside the body of the T-shirt. Use the fabric marker to draw a large rectangle on the front of the T-shirt. Draw more rectangles getting smaller and smaller inside the large rectangle.

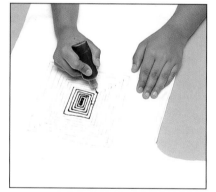

2 Go over the design with black pearl fabric paint in a squeeze bottle. If you are using a new bottle of pearl fabric paint, cut the nozzle close to the top. This will make it easy to paint fine lines.

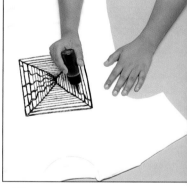

3 Paint lines with the black pearl fabric paint from each corner to the middle. This will divide the rectangle into four triangles. Then paint wiggly lines in the two side triangles with the black paint.

4 Divide each line in the bottom triangle into rectangles using the black pearl paint. The rectangles will get smaller as they get closer to the center. To finish your pattern, paint alternate rectangles black to make a checkered pattern.

HANDY HINT
This design is quite complicated, so it might be a good idea to practice it on a piece of paper. When you feel confident, draw the design on the T-shirt. To make straight lines, you can use a ruler.

Sunny Sunflower

On this bright T-shirt you can show off all your artistic flair for color, texture and shape. In fact, your painting will be so good that it will be framed in gold. There is only one thing missing from this painting—the signature of the talented artist.

YOU WILL NEED

Sheet of cardboard
Short-sleeved T-shirt
Fabric marker
Pot of water
Medium paintbrush

Fabric paint (black, yellow, red, orange light blue, gold)
Glitter fabric paint (gold)

1 Insert a piece of cardboard inside the body of the T-shirt. Use the fabric marker to draw the outline of the sunflower and the fancy picture frame.

2 Paint the center of the sunflower with black fabric paint. Use shades of yellow, red and orange to paint the petals. Let the paint dry.

3 Use sky blue fabric paint for the background of your sunflower painting. Take care not to paint over the petals or into the frame. Let the paint dry.

Using a clean brush, paint the picture frame with gold fabric [pa]int. For the final artistic touch, [de]corate the gilt frame with swirls [of] gold glitter fabric paint.

[H]ANDY HINT

[If y]ou splash fabric [pa]int on your clothes, [soa]k them immediately [in] lots of cold water. Keep [rin]sing them until the fabric [pa]int is removed. Then wash [the] clothes in warm, soapy water.

ACKNOWLEDGMENTS

The publishers would like to thank the following children for modeling for this book:

Nana Addae
Kristina Chase
Charlie Coulson
Reece Johnson
Alex Lindblom-Smith
Sophie Lindblom-Smith
Imran Miah
Lucy Nightingale
Tom Swaine Jameson
Sophie Viner

Thanks also to their parents and Walnut Tree Walk Primary School.

This book is dedicated to Lucy.